KENNETH COPELAND

◆

UNVEILING
YOUR REAL
SOURCE
OF
TROUBLE

Know Your Enemy

KENNETH

COPELAND

PUBLICATIONS

Unless otherwise noted, all scripture is from the *King James Version* of the Bible.

Scripture quotations marked *The Amplified Bible* and AMP are from *The Amplified Bible, Old Testament* © 1965, 1987 by The Zondervan Corporation. *The Amplified New Testament* © 1958, 1987 by The Lockman Foundation. Used by permission.

Know Your Enemy
Unveiling Your Real Source of Trouble
Previously published as *The Troublemaker*

ISBN-10 1-57562-629-2   30-0063
ISBN-13 978-1-57562-629-1

14 13 12 11 10 09   9 8 7 6 5 4

© 2002 Kenneth Copeland

Kenneth Copeland Publications
Fort Worth, TX 76192-0001

For more information about Kenneth Copeland Ministries, call 800-600-7395 or visit www.kcm.org.

TABLE OF
Contents

Kenneth Copeland

Once, when we were in Mexico, I went to a bullfight that left a lasting impression on me: The bull didn't know who his enemy was. He thought the red cape was his enemy. I remember thinking, *If he ever realizes his real source of trouble, that matador won't have a chance.*

As I travel among Christians everywhere, it is very evident to me that many believers are just like that poor bull. They are battling "red capes" instead of getting to the real source of their problems. They are contending against the trouble itself instead of *the troublemaker who is your enemy.*

Who is your enemy? Who is the real source of all of your troubles, whether they be spiritual, mental, physical, social or financial? If you knew, you would no longer struggle against the "red cape" of your problems. You would eliminate the very source of them. Just as that matador was no match for that mean, ferocious bull, the troublemaker is no match for the believer who battles him with the full armor and mighty weapons of God.

I have prepared this book to help you do just that. So, get ready. You're about to cause some serious trouble for your enemy!

CHAPTER ONE

Who Is Your Enemy?

Who Is Your Enemy?

Trouble seems to be as much of a part of life as breathing. Everyone has trouble at some point in his or her life. And human nature always wants to place the blame for its trouble on someone else. That started in the Garden of Eden. As soon as Adam had to explain his disobedience to God, he pointed the finger to his wife! When God said, "Adam, have you eaten from the forbidden tree?" Adam replied, "The woman that You gave me, *she* gave me of the tree and I ate! It wasn't *my* idea!" (The paraphrasing is mine.)

When trouble arises, the most natural thing to do is to place the blame for it on someone or something. Sadly, for the most part, many Christians have been falsely accusing God of being the cause of their troubles. This is the number one deception sown in the Church today—that our problems, our trials and our temptations are sent by God to teach us. This lie says that trials and tribulations are God's tools of developing and strengthening our character. The very extreme end of this deception is that God Himself is the author of our troubles or that God is the One Who makes us sick in order to teach us something.

> *The very basic principle of the Christian life is to know that God put our sin, sickness, disease, sorrow, grief and poverty on Jesus at Calvary.*

This is absolutely against the Word of God. Why? Because the very basic principle of the Christian life is to know that God put our sin, sickness, disease, sorrow, grief and poverty on Jesus at Calvary. For God to put any of this on us now to teach us or to strengthen our faith would be a miscarriage of justice. To believe that God has a purpose for your sickness would mean that Jesus bore your sicknesses in vain. What an insult to His love and care and compassion toward you!

In order to place blame where blame is due, believers need a fresh revelation of who is our true source of trouble. The only way we will receive this revelation is by rightly dividing the Word of Truth. James 1:8 says that a double-minded man is unstable in all his ways. Jesus said in Luke 11:17 that a house divided against itself will fall. Therefore, if a man thinks, imagines, assumes or in any way has the idea that God is behind his trouble—either by permission or commission—he will never resist it. And if he does not resist it, then he will certainly fail, because his hesitation will give Satan just the edge he needs to defeat him.

In the world of the spirit, there is a challenger, a counterfeit, an opponent of God who knows his business. But there is also the armor of

> *Believers need a fresh revelation of who is our true source of trouble.*

God, the Word of God and the power to defeat this opponent. The Bible says to resist Satan, and he will flee from you (James 4:7). But when a man hesitates—not opposing, but wondering—then Satan can easily defeat him. We must clearly distinguish between what is coming from Satan and not blame God for something that is not His doing. This is why it is so extremely important to rightly divide the Word concerning this issue.

Whenever God reveals His Word to a man, Satan comes immediately to steal the Word from his heart. Jesus said that he would. He said the sower sows the Word, and Satan comes immediately to take away the Word which was sown. (See Mark 4.)

Satan has no defense against the born-again believer who is walking in faith and acting on the Word of God.

Satan has no defense against the Word of God. He has no defense against the lordship of Jesus or the Name of Jesus. He has no defense against the born-again believer who is walking in faith and acting on the Word of God. He has no defense against these because Jesus said that *all* power has been given unto Him both in heaven and in earth (Matthew 28:18). Satan has been stripped of his power.

The devil knows he is defenseless, so in

order to stop the revelation of God's Word in the believer, his only tool is deception. He must sow a deception—something that sounds good and looks good but is really a wolf in sheep's clothing, He usually does this most successfully in the area of religion. He uses religion to blind and deceive the people. By sowing the seed of deception through religious tradition, Satan has robbed the Church of her power. He has no defense against our real spiritual weapons, but he can easily defend himself against our carnal, religious traditions.

Let's find out what God's Word has to say in the book of James about our troubles and shed the light on religious tradition.

My brethren, count it all joy when ye fall into divers temptations; Knowing this, that the trying of your faith worketh patience. But let patience have her perfect work, that ye may be perfect and entire, wanting nothing. If any of you lack wisdom, let him ask of God, that giveth to all men liberally, and upbraideth not; and it shall be given him. But let him ask in faith, nothing wavering. For he that wavereth is like a wave of the sea driven with the wind and tossed. For let not that man think that he shall receive any thing of the Lord. A double minded man is unstable in all his ways. (James 1:2-8)

Notice that James 1:3 says that the trying of your faith works patience. It does not say that the trying of your faith is to teach you, or that it *perfects* your faith, or that it makes your faith strong. Faith is strengthened by the Word of God. *"So then faith cometh by hearing, and hearing by the word of God"* (Romans 10:17). So, the trying of your faith exercises patience.

> *When we respond [with the Word], we take on the same attribute as Jesus.*

Now, what does *patience* mean? The definition of patience is not "to put up with" like many of us think. The dictionary says that to be *patient* is "to be constant, or the same way, all the time regardless of the circumstances."

This is the way we, as believers, must be—patient, stable, consistent, the same way all the time. Regardless of our circumstances, regardless of what life throws at us, we should always respond in exactly the same way: "Thus saith the Word of God!" When we respond this way, we take on the same attribute as Jesus—the same yesterday, today and forever. This is the reason Jesus is always the same—He never varies to the right or to the left from the Word of God.

James 1:4 tells us that, if we will let patience have her perfect work, we will be perfect and entire, wanting nothing. A patient man is a stable man. He is a constant man. He is a single-minded man. He doesn't have to ask himself, *Who is my enemy? Is God my problem or is Satan? Is there a shady area between the two?*

This poses another question many Christians are asking today. Does God use Satan to discipline His family? What *is* the chastisement of the Lord? Does it mean the same in the New Testament as it does in the Old?

To answer these questions, you must know how to rightly divide the Word of Truth.

Where do you rightly divide the Word? At the cross and resurrection of Jesus. One side is a promise—the other side is a fact.

Isaiah 53 is a prophecy of Jesus, the Messiah. Isaiah is prophesying here and is speaking of the things that are to be laid on Jesus. Notice verse 5:

> But he was wounded for our
> transgressions, he was bruised for
> our iniquities: the chastisement of
> our peace was upon him; and with
> his stripes we are healed.

The English dictionary defines *chastisement* as "punishment by inflicting pain." Jesus bore our sins so that we don't have to bear them. He bore our sicknesses so that we don't have to bear them. He bore our punishing chastisement so that we don't have to bear it. Praise God!

The following prophecy from Isaiah 54 is no longer speaking of Jesus on the cross. It is speaking of the Resurrected Jesus—the Redeemer. He is no longer speaking to Israel but to the Church of Jesus Christ.

In a little wrath I hid my face from
thee for a moment; but with everlasting
kindness will I have mercy on thee,
saith the Lord thy Redeemer...And all
thy children shall be taught of the Lord;
and great shall be the peace of thy children. In righteousness shalt thou be
established: thou shalt be far from
oppression; for thou shalt not fear:
and from terror, for it shall not come
near thee.

Behold, they shall surely gather
together, but not by me: whosoever
shall gather together against thee shall
fall for thy sake. Behold, I have created
the smith that bloweth the coals in the
fire, and that bringeth forth an instrument for his work; and I have created
the waster to destroy.

No weapon that is formed against
thee shall prosper, and every tongue that
shall rise against thee in judgment thou

shalt condemn. This is the heritage of
the servants of the Lord, and their righteousness is of me, saith the Lord.
(Isaiah 54:8, 13-17)

Notice in verse 8, *"but with everlasting
kindness will I have mercy on thee, saith the
Lord thy Redeemer."* The Redeemer is talking
here. When we read this, we are reading from
the mouth of God. This is what God Himself
has said.

*"And all thy children shall be taught of
the Lord; and great shall be the peace of thy
children."* Who are those children? We are.
The believers—the Body of Christ, the children of God as a result of the new birth.

*"In righteousness shalt thou be estab-
lished."* This is for us right now, here on
earth. We have already been established in
righteousness. Romans 5:17 says, *"For if by
one man's offence death reigned by one; much
more they which receive abundance of grace and
of the gift of righteousness shall reign in life by
one, Jesus Christ."*

"Thou shalt be far from oppression; for thou shalt not fear: and from terror; for it shall not come near thee." What does the Word say about us where fear is concerned? First John 2:5, *"But whoso keepeth his word, in him verily is the love of God perfected,"* and 1 John 4:18, *"There is no fear in love; but perfect love casteth out fear: because fear hath torment."*

"Behold, they shall surely gather together, but not by me: whosoever shall gather together against thee shall fall for thy sake." There is no question about it—oppression, fear, and terror will gather together against you. Satan will still try to fight you even though Jesus has defeated him through the cross. *"Behold, they shall surely gather together, **but not by me.**"* The Lord your Redeemer is speaking, and He says that oppression, fear and terror are **not** from Him.

"Behold, I have created the smith that bloweth the coals in the fire, and that bringeth forth an instrument for his work; and I have created the waster to destroy." What is the Lord saying here? God created

Satan. Ezekiel told of how Satan was created perfect, and then iniquity was found in him. This is where the problem lies. God has given His Word on certain indisputable points. He will not break or go back on His Word, even to Satan. This put God in the position of having to keep His Word when Satan became involved *and* keep His Word where man is involved. Satan is trying to trap God in a lie— to trap Him into going back on His Word. God would then be subject to the "father of liars." So what God is saying to us here is, "I created the one who caused your trouble. I will be responsible for it."

Satan is trying to trap God in a lie— to trap Him into going back on His Word.

"No weapon that is formed against thee shall prosper." Even though God created Satan, even though Satan committed treason before God and led man into treason, God has provided a way so that no weapon Satan forms against us will prosper.

"And every tongue that shall rise against thee in judgment thou shalt condemn. This

is the heritage of the servants of the Lord, and their righteousness is of me, saith the Lord." The battle lines are drawn. God is not your problem. Satan is your problem—he is your enemy. But the good news is that God has provided your complete deliverance through Jesus Christ.

The battle lines are drawn. God is not your problem. Satan is your problem.

CHAPTER TWO

God's Correction Through His Word

God's Correction Through His Word

We have seen that the word *chastisement* means "punishment by inflicting pain" and that Jesus bore our chastisement, or our punishment, with pain on the cross.

The Greek word translated *chastise* in the New Testament actually means "to instruct or to train." The question often arises, "How does God chastise His own?"

How *does* God instruct and train us? Does He unleash His bad dog to bite us on the leg, so we will learn to wear our boots? *No, He does not!*

For whom the Lord loveth he chasteneth, and scourgeth every son whom he receiveth. If ye endure chastening, God dealeth with you as with sons; for what son is he whom the father chasteneth not? But if ye be without chastisement, whereof all are partakers, then are ye bastards, and not sons.

Furthermore we have had fathers of our flesh which corrected us, and we gave them reverence: shall we not much rather be in subjection unto the Father of spirits, and live? (Hebrews 12:6-9)

Jesus said, *"That which is born of the flesh is flesh; and that which is born of the Spirit is spirit"* (John 3:6). Our fleshly fathers correct us in the flesh, but God is a spirit and He uses spiritual tools, not carnal tools. He uses spiritual weapons, not carnal weapons. Jesus said, "My *words* are spirit." He chastises with His words.

"For whom the Lord loveth he chasteneth." A loving God doesn't send tornadoes or cancer to His children. God never told me not to pray for someone's healing because He had put sickness on them. Jesus said, "If you've seen Me, you've seen the Father" (John 14:9). He never told a leper that he would have to keep leprosy so God could teach him something. The Word says in Acts 10:38, *"God anointed Jesus of Nazareth with the Holy Ghost and with power: who went about doing good, and healing all that were oppressed of the devil; for God was with him."* God did these things through Jesus. God is not double-minded—He is single-minded.

Now there are times when a situation looks as if God is behind it. It may have all the symptoms pointing to that. But Satan is a deceiver; he wants you to *think* God did it. If he can get you to go against God, he'll run rampant over you. The religious idea that God chastises His own with sickness and disease and poverty is the very thing that has caused the

> *A loving God does not send tornadoes or cancer to His children. . . . But Satan is a deceiver, he wants you to **think** God did it.*

Church to go 1,500 years without the knowledge of the Holy Spirit or the gifts of the Spirit.

We just became so passive, and double-minded
that the whole Church was schizophrenic,
except for a few men here and there who
refused to believe it—and most of them were
kicked out of their churches.

Now let's look at this a little closer. *"For
whom the Lord loveth he chasteneth, and
scourgeth every son whom he receiveth."* The
word *scourge* means "to beat on." God is the
Father of spirits. He doesn't scourge the flesh,
He scourges the inner man. How does He do
this? With His Word.

> *If Satan can get you
> to go against God,
> he'll run rampant
> over you.*

Every Scripture is God-breathed
(given by His inspiration) and profitable
for instruction, for reproof and conviction
of sin, for correction of error and discipline in obedience, and for training in
righteousness, So that the man of God
may be complete and proficient, well-
fitted and thoroughly equipped for every
good work. (2 Timothy 3:16-17, AMP)

The Lord chastises His own with the Scriptures. Put yourself in subjection to the Word. The Sword of the Spirit is two-edged—one side is for Satan and the other side is for you. It trims away the flesh and the lusts, and it sanctifies us.

I'll show you some examples of this. The Apostle Paul wrote in 2 Corinthians 7:8-9:

> For though I made you sorry with a letter, I do not repent, though I did repent: for I perceive that the same epistle hath made you sorry, though it were but for a season. Now I rejoice, not that ye were made sorry, but that ye sorrowed to repentance: for ye were made sorry after a godly manner.

God convicts, brings repentance, chastens and scourges us—with His Word.

This is the way in which God convicts, brings repentance, chastens, and scourges us—with His Word! He sent His Word to the church at Corinth, and it hurt so badly that they would have preferred being beaten with a stick! They knew how to handle sickness and disease, but when God reprimanded them with His Word, it cut deep into their spirits and they were sorry. Proverbs 17:10, *The Amplified Bible*, says, *"A reproof enters deeper into a man of understanding than a hundred lashes into a [self-confident] fool."*

When Peter preached the Word to the Jews on the Day of Pentecost, it pricked them in their hearts and they had to get saved. God does this with spirit-power, His Word. It chastens unbelief and purifies the human spirit in such a way that man comes out strong, not weak and condemned.

Daniel chastened himself before the Lord and asked the Lord to correct him. How did God correct him? He sent an angel to him and gave him His Word. God has done better than that for us. He hasn't sent us an angel— He has sent us the Holy Spirit to lead us into all the Truth. We need to fully understand the ministry of the Holy Spirit in the world today. Let's not take away from it. In other words, let's exercise our faith in this area. We need to realize that the Holy Spirit was sent here to teach the Church, to reveal the deep things of God to the Body of Christ. We need to develop our faith in the ability of the Holy Spirit to show us these things so that we might be *filled* with the knowledge of God in all wisdom and spiritual understanding.

You know, it seems that some people have an overwhelming desire to believe the worst from God. They will fight to prove that God is the one that inflicted them.

If you were to try talking this way about my earthly daddy, I'd fight you! Don't try to tell me that my dad lied to me or that he stole my property or made my babies sick. My father is a good man. He has worked hard to provide for me, and he would never lie to me. He loves me—he wouldn't hurt me—so don't try to tell me he's destroying my life!

I've heard people say something like this, "Well, God killed all my cattle and burned all my crops, but He finally got me down where He wanted me." No, God's not the one that did that! Your *earthly* father would never hurt you, so why do you want to believe that your *heavenly* Father would? James 1:13 says, *"Let no man say when he is tempted* [tested or tried], *I am tempted of God."*

How long are you going to listen when someone says, "God put that on you"?

I've heard people say, "Well, look what God did to Job!" What *did* God do to Job? He built a hedge around him and blessed him with abundance. At the end of the book of James, the Word says that God was full of pity and mercy in His dealings with Job.

For years now, we've read about Job and have blamed God for Job's situation, thinking that God commissioned Satan to attack Job. That's not true! In Job 1, Satan came to God and said, "Put your hand against Job, and he will curse you." He tried to get God to do it, but God would not. He said, "Behold [look and see], he is in your power." Job was already in Satan's power by letting that hedge fall from around him. He quit acting in faith, began operating in fear, and that protective hedge fell.

Then he was vulnerable to Satan's attack. The sacrifices he made were not made in faith. The Word says he made the same ones continually (Job 1:5). He lost everything he had. Job didn't have the written Word of God to act on like you and I do today. He said, "That which I have so greatly feared has come upon me" (Job 3:25).

Then he began by trial and error to figure a way to get back his faith again. He tried crying about it, he tried cutting and hurting himself, he sat down in the ashes—none of this did him any good at all. Satan sent him some very religious men, and they certainly didn't help him! They were the ones that said God had done it. God Himself told these men, however, that they had not spoken of Him rightly.

But the very moment Job moved back in faith by praying for those men, he moved back on the Word of God and God replaced double everything he had lost. When Job began operating in faith once again, his deliverance was instantaneous.

We need to preach *this* instead of identifying with Job's sickness and failure. People say,

"Well, I'm just like poor old Job." We'll, if you're going to be like Job, then you will have to get healed and delivered. Job wasn't poor either—he was the richest man in the East when this began and then God doubled that! All God has ever done and all He has ever said has been deliverance, freedom and power for His people.

If you're going to be like Job, then you will have to get healed and delivered.

I refuse to believe that my heavenly Father would hurt me, even though I may not know all the circumstances. It may look as though He is behind it, but I refuse to fall for that. I know He sent His Son to die for me, so I'm not going to hesitate for one moment and give Satan the opportunity to move in on me.

Trouble-preaching—being trouble-centered and trouble-minded instead of being victory-minded—will give Satan just the moment's hesitation he needs to defeat you.

CHAPTER THREE

The Protective Umbrella of God's Will

The Protective Umbrella of God's Will

There is one particular area in which the Body of Christ has been trouble-minded for a long time. We have taken one verse of Scripture, lifted it out of context, and misused it terribly. In Romans 8:28 the Apostle Paul wrote this, *"And we know that all things work together for good to them that love God, to them who are the called according to his purpose."* You have probably heard this quoted over and over again in the light of trouble.

All the way through Romans 8, Paul is talking about the difference between the law of death and the law of life—that these are two different laws. He tells us that we are not governed by the law of death, we have been delivered from it. *"The law of the Spirit of life in Christ Jesus hath made me free from the law of sin and death"* (Romans 8:2). He shows us the difference between being carnally minded (or flesh-minded) and being spiritually minded (or Word-minded). He says, *"For to be carnally minded is death; but to be spiritually minded is life and peace"* (Romans 8:6). There is the division between the two. You can't be trouble-minded and spiritually minded at the same time. Trouble isn't born by the Spirit of God—it is born by Satan.

Now, look at Romans 8:26, *"Likewise the Spirit also helpeth our infirmities: for we know not what we should pray for as we ought: but the Spirit itself maketh intercession for us."*

> *Trouble isn't born by the Spirit of God—it is born by Satan.*

The Spirit of God is not interceding *for us*—He is helping us to intercede. That's His ministry. The Holy Spirit leads us and takes up where we fall short of spiritual knowledge. The word translated *helpeth* actually is three Greek words combined. It literally says "takes hold together with us against." This verse literally reads, "The Spirit takes hold together with us against our infirmities."

> For we know not what we should pray for as we ought: but the Spirit itself maketh intercession for us with groanings which cannot be uttered. And he that searcheth the hearts knoweth what is the mind of the Spirit, because he maketh intercession for the saints according to the will of God. And we know that all things work together for good to them that love God, to them who are the called according to his purpose. For whom he did foreknow, he also did predestinate to be conformed to the image of his Son, that he might be the firstborn among many brethren. (Romans 8:26-29)

The Apostle Paul is talking here about intercessory prayer—how it works, how it operates. By being trouble-minded, we have subconsciously read verse 28 like this: "For we know that all **bad** things work together for the good of those that love God." But it doesn't say that at all! It wasn't talking about bad things—it was talking about good things—about intercessory prayer.

He says in verse 29, *"he also did predestinate to be conformed to the image of his Son."* What tools does the Holy Spirit use to conform us to the image of His Son? The nine gifts of the Spirit, the Name of Jesus, the blood of the Lamb, the Word of God, and everything that the New Testament guarantees the believer in this life and in the world to come. When the believer begins to move into intercession, when he begins to intercede for the Body of Christ as he should, then these tools come together and operate against our infirmities, so we pray accurately and powerfully by the anointing of the Holy Spirit. In this way, all these things work together for the good of those that love God.

COUNT IT ALL JOY

The Word tells us to *"count it all joy when we fall into divers temptations"* (James 1:2) or, as the Greek text says, "into different trials and tribulations." What does the Word say about joy? There is a difference between joy and happiness. Happiness is controlled by the condition or the comfort of the five physical senses. Joy is not. The Bible says that joy is a fruit of the spirit. It is a spiritual force—it is born inside the human heart. We read in Nehemiah 8:10 that the joy of the Lord is our strength, so we can count it strength when these trials and tribulations come our way. Don't count it defeat—count it strength! Don't count it negative—count it affirmative! Jesus said, *"Ask, and ye shall receive, that your joy may be full"* (John 16:24). Count it answered prayer.

To *count it all joy* does not mean that you are to thank God *because* your child is sick. Let's look at a portion of the Scripture here that is often misunderstood.

Rejoice evermore. Pray without ceasing. In every thing give thanks: for this is the will of God in Christ Jesus concerning you. (1 Thessalonians 5:16-18)

Some of us have read this verse and thought, "The will of God is for me to give thanks for everything." That is not true. That *thing* or *circumstance* is not the will of God for you—*giving thanks* is the will of God. When you praise God and give Him thanks in the midst of your situation, you step under the protective umbrella of the will of God. You may not know what the Word says about your particular situation, but the Word *does* say to give thanks. Then, while you are under that protective umbrella, Satan can't touch you.

You may ask, "How do you count it all joy, Brother Copeland?" I had a good opportunity to do this one night when my little daughter had a high fever. I went into her room, laid hands on

> *When you are under [God's] protective power, Satan can't touch you.*

her and prayed, "Father, in the Name of Jesus, I count it all joy to prove once again that the Word is real and filled with power. I'm a faith man, and I'm not moved by what I see. I'm turning her over to You, and I believe that You will take care of her in Jesus' Name. Now, I just praise You and thank You for her healing." I didn't praise God for her fever because it wasn't hers and God didn't give it to her. Jesus bore her sickness and disease. If it belonged to anyone, it belonged to Satan, who was trying to put it on her.

I have accepted Calvary as the sacrifice that paid the price for my total redemption— from sin, sickness, poverty, and death. I believe that and I stand on it. I have certain rights, called righteousness, in the kingdom of God and one of these is the right to a healthy body. Jesus has provided it for me, and I take hold of it with my faith.

CHAPTER FOUR

Use
Your
Authority!

Use Your Authority!

What about the question of whether or not God permits bad things to happen to us? The answer to that is yes, He does permit them. There isn't much He can do about it! Why? Because we have been given authority in the earth. God gave Adam the authority to rule the earth, to have dominion over it, and to subdue it. God didn't butt in on man's business after that. He kept His Word with Adam, even though He had to swear to His own hurt to keep it. Did God send the devil in to get Adam? No, He kicked out the devil and gave Adam authority over the whole situation. Adam was the one that let in the devil. Jesus said, "All power has been given unto me, both in heaven and on earth, so you go into all the world and preach the gospel. In my Name, cast out the devil" (Matthew 28:18; Mark 16:15-18). He gave the believer His Word and the commission to do it. There should be no hesitation, nothing dubious about our thinking.

We have been given authority in the earth, and when we let the thief run loose, there is nothing God can do about it. A city judge has legal authority, but if the policemen out in the field just let the thief run loose and never get him to the judge, then there's nothing the judge or the law can do about it. It's the man out in the field with authority to make arrests that makes the difference between law and order and a riot. You and I, as believers, are God's policemen in the field. We have the authority of the Name of Jesus and the Sword of the Spirit. There is no reason why Satan should run roughshod over any born-again believer.

> *We have been given authority in the earth, and when we let the thief run loose, there is nothing God can do about it.*

With every situation and every circumstance, we must make a very definite choice.
Notice Deuteronomy 30:19:

> I call heaven and earth to record
> this day against you, that I have set
> before you life and death, blessing and
> cursing: therefore choose life, that both
> thou and thy seed may live.

The choice is yours—either life or death,
blessing or cursing. God has set this choice
before you with His written Word. The only
way you can find the true definitions of life
and death is by studying His Word.

Jesus said, "My words are life" (John
6:63). God told Joshua that if he would medi-
tate in the Word day and night, he would
prosper and have good success. Proverbs
4:20-22 tells us to attend to the words of
God *"for they are life unto those that find them,
and health to all their flesh."*

In order to choose life and blessing, you
will have to choose the Word of God, for it is

life. You will have to become Word-minded instead of trouble-minded, life-minded instead of death-minded. You will have to become single-minded on the Word of God. When you become Word-minded, you begin to realize that He Who raised Jesus from the dead is residing in you and He that is in you is greater than he that is in the world.

The dividing line between life and death is this: The thief, Satan, comes only to kill, steal and to destroy. Jesus came that we might have life and have it more abundantly (John 10:10).

> *The dividing line between life and death is this: Satan comes only to kill, steal and destroy. Jesus came that we might have life and have it more abundantly.*

Satan is the thief. He is trying to rob the Body of Christ of its power. The believer has the whole armor of God available to him, and Satan has no defense for that armor. He must deceive the believer and sidetrack him. He must operate in the world of the natural because in the world of the spirit, the believer can beat him with his powerful spiritual weapons. The Sword of the Spirit, God's Word, can wound Satan deeply, so he uses deception.

He comes against the believer in the physical world and tries to convince him that God is actually the one who made him sick or that God took his baby or that God wants him to live in poverty. If the believer entertains those thoughts for any length of time, he will begin to doubt. He will hesitate. He will become double-minded. That hesitation will give Satan a valuable advantage. Then the next time Satan attacks, that believer will be a little easier to defeat.

The believer must decide not to back up any longer. The man that is single-minded on God's Word has to know for sure that God's will was Jesus on the Cross; that God's will is for him to prosper and be in health; that God's will is to meet all his needs according to His riches in glory by Christ Jesus; that God's will is for him to receive the blessings of Abraham through faith in Jesus Christ.

When these facts become a reality on the inside of him, then he becomes a powerful believer, a joint heir with Jesus Christ. He knows that his Father has carefully planned for his deliverance and for his victory. From that point forward, he'll never question whether or not he should prosper or whether or not he ought to be healed. He is no longer on the defense—he is on the attack. He no longer hesitates—he is constant and stable.

Jesus said He would build His Church on the rock and the gates of hell would not prevail against it (Matthew 16:18). In other words, the powers of hell would not succeed against it. That rock is the Word of God. Jesus compared the man who acts on the Word to a man who built his house on the rock (Matthew 7:24). When the storm beat against the house, it stood strong. In this parable the storm beat against both houses—the one on the rock and the one on the sand. The same storm hit both houses. It wasn't the storm that made the house strong. The house was strong *before* the storm hit. It was built on a firm foundation. This is how the Body of Christ is to be—built on the firm foundation of the Word of God.

Become single-minded. Make the decision—choose life and blessing. Decide to win—decide to overcome. Until this decision is made, you will be double-minded. But the moment you make your decision to be a winner, you will be out on top! There will be times when you'll have to stand and be patient and consistent, but when a man is consistent on the Word of God, he will know the Truth and the Truth will make him free.

CHAPTER FIVE

Maintain a Winning Attitude

Maintain a Winning Attitude

While preaching the gospel across this country, I have realized one main thing the Lord is saying to His people: God is a winner—He is not a failure. Consequently, His people are winners and not failures. We are to have a victorious attitude in Christ!

In Ephesians 4:23, the Apostle Paul told the Church to have the spirit of their minds renewed. In other words, they should have their whole attitude renewed. We need to renew our minds to the Word of God—to the fact that Jesus has overcome the world.

We've all heard it said, "It's not whether you win or lose, it's how you play the game." That is nonsense! *If you play the game right,*

you'll win! There is no substitute for being a
winner. Man was created as a dominating lord.
He was given dominion over the earth and
everything that crept, flew, crawled and
breathed in the earth. Man is a winner—he
does not know how to graciously accept
defeat. When he accepts defeat and failure as
his lot in life, he lowers himself, not only
below other principalities and powers, but he
lowers himself below the devil and even below
the animal kingdom.

I'm reminded here of something George
Patton said as a general in the Army of the
United States. He was a great commander with
a God-given insight into war. (You might ask:
"Does God give men insight into war?" Yes.
Look at David—God showed him how to
fight. There are some men called of God to
handle the garbage jobs—the blood-and-guts
jobs—that have to be done. Many times these
jobs have been glorified by men, but they are
not glorious jobs!) George Patton was one of
these garbage men. He knew how to win a war
and said it this way: "Some of you men have

come with your minds made up to die for your country. That's not the way to win a war! The way to win a war is to make your enemies die for theirs!" He had his mind made up to win—and dying wasn't the way to do it. That man had a winning attitude.

As believers we need to develop that kind of winning attitude.

> Whosoever believeth that Jesus is the Christ is born of God: and every one that loveth him that begat loveth him also that is begotten of him. By this we know that we love the children of God, when we love God, and keep his commandments. For this is the love of God, that we keep his commandments: and his commandments are not grievous. For whatsoever is born of God overcometh the world: and this is the victory that overcometh the world, even our faith. Who is he that overcometh the world, but he that believeth that Jesus is the Son of God? (1 John 5:1-5)

Now God is being unusually explanatory here. He normally does not explain things written in the Word of God this deeply for a very good reason: He intends for us to take what He says by faith, go to Him and allow the Holy Spirit to reveal it to our hearts. This way He doesn't tip the devil to what it means. God wrote the Bible as a code book. Proverbs says that God has hidden godly wisdom for His people. This is the way He wants it. But here in this portion of Scripture, God goes an unusual step further and asks the question, "Who is he that overcometh the world?" In other words, God is saying, "This is the way I see this—whatsoever is born of Me overcomes the world; and who is he that overcomes the world, but he who believes that Jesus is the Christ, the Son of the living God?"

Now this can be read another way: "Nobody but those who believe that Jesus is the Christ will ever overcome the world." This world will not be overcome by a government, by a political system, or by a monetary system. Money will *never* overcome the world! When the Bible talks about "the world," it is speaking of the dominion of darkness, the god of this world, the evil spirit—Satan—that operates in the world. No man or system will ever—in any way, form or fashion—overcome the world without Jesus Christ as Lord. You'll never be able to do it unless you're born of Him. But on the other hand, if you are *born* of Him, you have an absolute, perfect, God-given, blood-bought right to overcome every aspect of the world—everything it could possibly send your way!

> *No man or system will ever—in any way, form or fashion— overcome the world without Jesus Christ as Lord.*

Let's consider this question again. This is what we must grasp. Who is he that overcomes the world? He who believes that Jesus is the Christ. Do you believe that Jesus is the Christ, the Son of the Living God? If so, then you have committed yourself to overcoming the world. If you believe the Word of God, then your attitude should be, "Well, praise God, I'm an overcomer!" This should be your attitude regardless of what comes against you.

Jesus said in John 16:33:

These things I have spoken unto
you, that in me ye might have peace.
In the world ye shall have tribulation:
but be of good cheer; I have overcome
the world.

In other words, Jesus is saying, "The world
will come at you with everything it has to offer,
but don't worry about it—I've already beaten
it—I've already overcome the world." Jesus was
not referring to just 99 percent of the world.
He said, "I have overcome **the world**." One
hundred percent of it! It makes no difference
what the world throws at you, you can turn to
Jesus because He has already overcome it.

Now notice He said, *"that in me ye might
have peace."* Jesus was teaching here about
being one with Him and being one with the
Father. He was telling His disciples that soon
the Holy Spirit would come and do things they
could not then understand. They couldn't
grasp what it meant to be "in Him." Without

the Holy Spirit today, none of us could under-stand this. It takes the Holy Spirit to reveal these things—particularly the reality of being born again. Jesus told Nicodemus about it, but he could only think of a man going back into his mother's womb. Jesus told him, "I'm speaking of heavenly things, and you don't even understand earthly things" (John 3:13).

These men had no concept of what Jesus was about to do at Calvary. They had no idea that through His death and Resurrection, He was to become the firstborn from the dead and issue forth a new race of men who are, in God, born again and filled with the mighty Spirit of God Himself. They could not conceive this when He was on the Cross, nor even after He was raised from the dead. Only after the Holy Spirit came on the Day of Pentecost could they see what Jesus had been saying. Then Peter stood up and boldly preached the Word of God by revelation of the Holy Ghost. Can you see the change in his life?

So Jesus teaches His men and then He prays for them. John 17:1, *"These words spake*

Jesus, and lifted up his eyes to heaven, and said, Father." Let's look at some of the things He prayed. Verse 13, *"And now come I to thee; and these things I speak in the world, that they might have my joy fulfilled in themselves."*

Verse 15, *"I pray not that thou shouldest take them out of the world, but that thou shouldest keep them from the evil."* You see, we are to live *above* the evil in the world. This ties in with what He said earlier— that we would have tribula-tion in the world, but to be of good cheer, because He has overcome the world. Then He prays the prayer which is the basis for the way God causes us to live above the evil in the world— above the trials and tests and tribulations.

> *The Word is your sword. Fight with it.*

Verse 17, *"Sanctify them through thy truth: thy word is truth."*

Verse 20, *"Neither pray I for these alone, but for them also which shall believe on me through their word."* He was praying here for you and me. He said, "I'm not praying just for these before Me, but also for everybody that believes on Me through their word."

All of us received Jesus as Lord by the word of one or more of these disciples—either directly or indirectly. Jesus was praying that prayer for you. What did He pray? "Separate them with Your Word." The Word of God will separate you from the world. The Word is your sword. Fight with it. It will fight its own fight. Notice verse 18, *"As thou hast sent me into the world, even so have I also sent them into the world."*

Verses 20-21:

Neither pray I for these alone, but for them also which shall believe on me through their word; That they all may be one; as thou, Father, art in me, and I in thee, that they also may be one in us: that the world may believe that thou hast sent me.

Notice that Jesus said, "We're all going to be one." The Apostle Paul said in 1 Corinthians 6:17, *"But he that is joined unto the Lord is one spirit."* Another translation says, *"But he that is joined unto the Lord is one spirit with Him."* The Bible also says we are bone of His bone, and we just read that anyone who believes Jesus is the Christ is born of God.

We are to be conformed to the very attitude of God. We are to take His innermost feelings, place them in our hearts and cause our wills and attitudes to conform to His. But the only way we will get them is by acting on the Word. This is a much higher calling and a greater form of life than just submitting ourselves to God. We are to have our attitudes changed to completely and absolutely conform to the Son of the Living God.

The Word says we are predestined to be conformed to His very image. It says we are one with Him—one spirit with Him. It says we have the mind of Christ, and we are bone of His bone. Thank God, we're connected to Jesus—spirit, soul and body—through the Holy Spirit and by His Word. We are completely and totally ONE with Him, so let's put ourselves in God's position for a moment.

Is there any part of your life God can't handle? Certainly not!

Have you ever caught God asleep? No, the Bible says He never slumbers.

Have you ever gone to Jesus with a problem He didn't know how to solve? No.

Have you ever heard Jesus say, "Well, I thought I had overcome the world, but evidently, I haven't." No, you have not!

Well, we're one with Him. If that's His attitude, then praise God, it should be our attitude. We are overcomers with Him!

Jesus said in Matthew 19:26, "All things are possible with God," everyone would smile and quickly agree, but the same Bible, the same Jesus, the same Word of God says, "All things are possible to him that believes" (Mark 9:23). If you believe the first statement, then you have to believe the second.

You and I need to change our perspective in all of this. We are one with Him, so we need to set our attitude to match His attitude. If we are one with Him in the spirit, one with Him in mind, and one with Him in body, then we ought to be one with Him in attitude as well!

What is Jesus' attitude? A good example is

the Lord's Prayer (Matthew 6:9-13). Jesus did not pray this for Himself or anyone else. It was simply an example of His attitude of prayer. He makes some outright confessions of faith.

"Our Father which art in heaven, Hallowed be thy name. Thy kingdom come. Thy will be done in earth, as it is in heaven" (Matthew 6:9-10). This is a statement of faith. It shows His winning attitude. He was standing there in the face of people that wanted to hang Him! He didn't say, "Father, if it be Your will."

He didn't just say, "Thy will be done." He said, "Your will be done in earth *as it is in heaven!*" Is there sickness and poverty and suffering in heaven? No! Then there shouldn't be any of that here on earth. Can you see His attitude in this? God doesn't have sickness in heaven, so He doesn't want any here on the earth!

God doesn't have any sickness in heaven, so He doesn't want any here on the earth!

Our attitude needs to be the same as His. Jesus is the Eternal Winner—He is always a winner! God can tell you what will happen

6,000 years from now. Why? Because the events taking place in the next 6,000 years or the next 6,000,000 years will not happen by chance. They are established. Where? In the mind of God. He has faith operating in His own ability. He is a faith being. He can tell you what will happen in the future because He intends for it to come out that way! He can give you His wisdom because it's going to be the way He decides.

How does He do it? With His faith. He doesn't expect to fail. He doesn't prepare to fail. Satan will get in and try to destroy things, but God doesn't worry—He knows it will come out all right. That's how we are to be. Roll all your cares over on Him. Don't be moved by what you feel or by what you see. You're a faith man, so you know how things are going to come out. You're going to win! Praise God!

CHAPTER SIX

See Yourself as God Sees You

See Yourself as God Sees You

The Church—the Body of Christ—has lived far below her privileges. We have lived as far below our spiritual privileges as Israel has lived below her political privileges. Israel should be the head and not the tail. She should not have to borrow from any nation on earth, and every nation on earth should be in debt to her. That's what God said. Well, that's how far below our spiritual privileges the Body of Christ has lived.

Down through the years, God exercised His faith for us. He was willing to work over 2,000 years to get His plan functioning properly.

The whole time the world lay in darkness, God was still believing—still exercising faith— not in Himself alone but in you and in me. Ephesians 4:14-16 tells us:

> That we henceforth be no more children, tossed to and fro, and carried about with every wind of doctrine, by the sleight of men, and cunning craftiness, whereby they lie in wait to deceive; But speaking the truth in love, may grow up into him in all things, which is the head, even Christ: From whom the whole body fitly joined together and compacted by that which every joint supplieth, according to the effectual working in the measure of every part...

God did not say He would hold the Body of Christ together. He said He would join it together, but that it would be held together, or compacted, by that which every joint supplied. He had to believe that you and I would supply what it took to hold the Body together. We failed and we failed and we failed again, but God kept on joining and believing. He never would utter words of failure. Theology cried, "The Church is failing!" God said, "My house will be full, and the gates of hell will not prevail against it!" Religion was failing—God wasn't! Can you see His attitude?

"Compacted by that which every joint supplieth, according to the effectual working in the measure of every part." In other words, it works according to the effect brought about by the direct amount, or the measure, that each and every joint supplies. The amount which you supply—the power you supply—affects the entire plan of God. Whatever you supply—none, some, much, or all you're called to do—affects the entire Body of Christ.

> *The amount which you supply affects the entire plan of God.*

"According to the effectual working in the measure of every part, maketh increase of the body unto the edifying of itself in love." Here again, God will not build up the Body—it must build up itself. Some people are waiting for Jesus to return so that the Body will rise

without spot or wrinkle at the resurrection.
But the Body of Christ is rising now, and the
Bible says He will present Himself a body that
is without spot or wrinkle. This will happen as
she edifies herself in love, grows up into Him
and is washed of water by the Word.

Can you see how God's faith was operating
through the years? The Word of God had been
written long before the Dark Ages, yet because
it was inaccessible to the people, most could
not get born again. It had been shoved deep
into monasteries, and they couldn't reach it.
But God kept believing. There was enough
faith in God's winning attitude to reach a little
Catholic priest named Martin Luther. That little priest began to scratch in the Word and he
found a sentence, *"The just shall live by faith"*
(Romans 1:17). He found God through that
one little sentence and generated enough
power to begin a revival that is still going! God
had a winning attitude, and He refused to let
go! Today the gospel is being preached in every
nation on the face of the earth!

You're one with Him in the spirit, you have

the mind of Christ, you are bone of His bone, so you might as well be attitude of His attitude! His attitude is *"Thy will be done in earth, as it is in heaven."* See yourself as God sees you.

One time the Lord showed me a vision of a man holding a big banana. The man began to peel the banana, and as he did, I saw that there was no banana inside, but standing in the bottom was a little man. That little man was me! The Lord said, *Son, that's your attitude toward yourself.* It was true. I presented a big front to the world, but actually felt very small on the inside. The Lord told me I needed to change my whole attitude.

He began to show me from His Word what it meant to be *in Christ* and to have Him in me. I began to see that a born-again believer is a limitless creature of God—an unlimited powerhouse of the very life of God Himself!

You, too, need to change your attitude by renewing your mind to the Word. Allow God to reveal Himself to you and to give you this winning attitude—this world-overcoming attitude—in Jesus Christ.

Now that you see that God is not your problem and that you have the very power of God at your disposal to make you an overcomer, you are in the position to be more trouble than your troublemaker—Satan—can handle! Now, you can put Satan under your feet where he belongs.

PRAYER FOR SALVATION AND BAPTISM IN THE HOLY SPIRIT

Heavenly Father, I come to You in the Name of Jesus. Your Word says, "Whosoever shall call on the name of the Lord shall be saved" (Acts 2:21). I am calling on You. I pray and ask Jesus to come into my heart and be Lord over my life according to Romans 10:9-10: "If thou shalt confess with thy mouth the Lord Jesus, and shalt believe in thine heart that God hath raised him from the dead, thou shalt be saved. For with the heart man believeth unto righteousness; and with the mouth confession is made unto salvation." I do that now. I confess that Jesus is Lord, and I believe in my heart that God raised Him from the dead.

I am now reborn! I am a Christian—a child of Almighty God! I am saved! You also said in Your Word, "If ye then, being evil, know how to give good gifts unto your children: HOW MUCH MORE shall your heavenly Father give the Holy Spirit to them that ask him?" (Luke 11:13). I'm also asking You to fill me with the Holy Spirit. Holy Spirit, rise up within me as I praise God. I fully expect to speak with other tongues as You give me the utterance (Acts 2:4). In Jesus' Name. Amen!

Begin to praise God for filling you with the Holy Spirit. Speak those words and syllables you receive—not in your own language, but the language given to you by the Holy Spirit. You have to use your own voice. God will not force you to speak. Don't be concerned with how it sounds. It is a heavenly language!

Continue with the blessing God has given you and pray in the spirit every day.

You are a born-again, Spirit-filled believer. You'll never be the same!

Find a good church that boldly preaches God's Word and obeys it. Become part of a church family who will love and care for you as you love and care for them.

We need to be connected to each other. It increases our strength in God. It's God's plan for us.

Make it a habit to watch the *Believer's Voice of Victory* television broadcast and become a doer of the Word, who is blessed in his doing (James 1:22-25).

About the Author

Kenneth Copeland is co-founder and president of Kenneth Copeland Ministries in Fort Worth, Texas, and best-selling author of books that include *How to Discipline Your Flesh* and *Honor—Walking in Honesty, Truth and Integrity*.

Now in his 41st year as a minister of the gospel of Christ and teacher of God's Word, Kenneth is the recording artist of such award-winning albums as his Grammy-nominated *Only the Redeemed, In His Presence, He Is Jehovah, Just a Closer Walk* and his most recently released *Big Band Gospel* album. He also co-stars as the character Wichita Slim in the children's adventure videos *The Gunslinger, Covenant Rider* and the movie *The Treasure of Eagle Mountain,* and as Daniel Lyon in the *Commander Kellie and the Superkids*SM videos *Armor of Light* and *Judgment: The Trial of Commander Kellie.*

With the help of offices and staff in the United States, Canada, England, Australia, South Africa and Ukraine, Kenneth is fulfilling his vision to boldly preach the uncompromised Word of God from the top of this world, to the bottom, and all the way around. His ministry reaches millions of people worldwide through daily and Sunday TV broadcasts, magazines, teaching audios and videos, conventions and campaigns, and the World Wide Web.

by Kenneth Copeland

*   A Ceremony of Marriage
    A Matter of Choice
    Covenant of Blood
    Faith and Patience—The Power Twins
*   Freedom From Fear
    Giving and Receiving
    Honor—Walking in Honesty, Truth and Integrity
    How to Conquer Strife
    How to Discipline Your Flesh
    How to Receive Communion
    In Love There Is No Fear
    Know Your Enemy
    Living at the End of Time—A Time of
       Supernatural Increase
    Love Letters From Heaven
    Love Never Fails
*   Mercy—The Divine Rescue of the Human Race
*   Now Are We in Christ Jesus
    One Nation Under God (gift book with CD enclosed)
*   Our Covenant With God
    Partnership—Sharing the Vision, Sharing the Grace
*   Prayer—Your Foundation for Success
*   Prosperity: The Choice Is Yours
    Rumors of War
*   Sensitivity of Heart
*   Six Steps to Excellence in Ministry
*   Sorrow Not! Winning Over Grief and Sorrow
*   The Decision Is Yours
*   The Force of Faith
*   The Force of Righteousness
    The Image of God in You
    The Laws of Prosperity
    The Outpouring of the Spirit—
       The Result of Prayer
*   The Power of the Tongue
    The Power to Be Forever Free
*   The Winning Attitude

*Available in Spanish

Turn Your Hurts Into Harvests
Walking in the Realm of the Miraculous
* Welcome to the Family
* You Are Healed!
Your Right-Standing With God

by Gloria Copeland

* And Jesus Healed Them All
Are You Listening?
Are You Ready?
Be a Vessel of Honor
Blessed Beyond Measure
Build Your Financial Foundation
Fight On!
God Has Your Miracle on His Mind
God's Master Plan for Your Life
God's Prescription for Divine Health
God's Success Formula
God's Will for You
God's Will for Your Healing
God's Will Is Prosperity
* God's Will Is the Holy Spirit
Go With the Flow
* Harvest of Health
* Hearing From Heaven
Hidden Treasures
Living in Heaven's Blessings Now
Looking for a Receiver
* Love—The Secret to Your Success
No Deposit—No Return
Pleasing the Father
Pressing In—It's Worth It All
Shine On!
The Grace That Makes Us Holy
The Power to Live a New Life
The Protection of Angels
There Is No High Like the Most High
The Secret Place of God's Protection (gift book with CD enclosed)
The Unbeatable Spirit of Faith
This Same Jesus
To Know Him
True Prosperity
Walk With God

Well Worth the Wait
Words That Heal (gift book with CD enclosed)
Your Promise of Protection—The Power of the 91st Psalm

Books Co-Authored by Kenneth and Gloria Copeland

Family Promises
Healing Promises
Prosperity Promises
Protection Promises

* From Faith to Faith—A Daily Guide to Victory
From Faith to Faith—A Perpetual Calendar
He Did It All for You
One Word From God Can Change Your Life

One Word From God Series:
• One Word From God Can Change Your Destiny
• One Word From God Can Change Your Family
• One Word From God Can Change Your Finances
• One Word From God Can Change Your Formula for Success
• One Word From God Can Change Your Health
• One Word From God Can Change Your Nation
• One Word From God Can Change Your Prayer Life
• One Word From God Can Change Your Relationships

Load Up—A Youth Devotional
Over the Edge—A Youth Devotional
Pursuit of His Presence—A Daily Devotional
Pursuit of His Presence—A Perpetual Calendar
Raising Children Without Fear

Other Books Published by KCP

John G. Lake—His Life, His Sermons, His
    Boldness of Faith
The Holiest of All by Andrew Murray
The New Testament in Modern Speech by
    Richard Francis Weymouth
The Rabbi From Burbank by Isidor Zwirn and Bob Owen
Unchained! by Mac Gober

*Available in Spanish

Products Designed for Today's Children and Youth

And Jesus Healed Them All (confession book and CD gift package)
Baby Praise Board Book
Baby Praise Christmas Board Book
Noah's Ark Coloring Book
The Best of *Shout!* Adventure Comics
The *Shout!* Giant Flip Coloring Book
The *Shout!* Joke Book
The *Shout!* Super-Activity Book
Wichita Slim's Campfire Stories

*Commander Kellie and the Superkids*_{SM} Books:

The SWORD Adventure Book
*Commander Kellie and the Superkids*_{SM} Solve-It-Yourself Mysteries
*Commander Kellie and the Superkids*_{SM} Adventure Series:
Middle Grade Novels by Christopher P.N. Maselli:

#1 The Mysterious Presence
#2 The Quest for the Second Half
#3 Escape From Jungle Island
#4 In Pursuit of the Enemy
#5 Caged Rivalry
#6 Mystery of the Missing Junk
#7 Out of Breath
#8 The Year Mashela Stole Christmas
#9 False Identity
#10 The Runaway Mission
#11 The Knight-Time Rescue of Commander Kellie

WORLD OFFICES
KENNETH COPELAND MINISTRIES

For more information about KCM and our products,
please write to the office nearest you:

Kenneth Copeland Ministries
Fort Worth, TX 76192-0001

Kenneth Copeland
Locked Bag 2600
Mansfield Delivery Centre
QUEENSLAND 4122
AUSTRALIA

Kenneth Copeland
Private Bag X 909
FONTAINEBLEAU
2032
REPUBLIC OF
SOUTH AFRICA

Kenneth Copeland Ministries
Post Office Box 84
L'VIV 79000
UKRAINE

Kenneth Copeland
Post Office Box 15
BATH
BA1 3XN
U.K.

Kenneth Copeland
PO Box 3111 STN LCD 1
Langley BC V3A 4R3
CANADA

WE'RE HERE FOR YOU!

Believer's Voice of Victory Television Broadcast

Join Kenneth and Gloria Copeland and the *Believer's Voice of Victory* broadcasts Monday through Friday and on Sunday each week, and learn how faith in God's Word can take your life from ordinary to extraordinary. This teaching from God's Word is designed to get you where you want to be—*on top!*

You can catch the *Believer's Voice of Victory* broadcast on your local, cable or satellite channels.* Also available 24 hours on webcast at BVOV.TV.

   * Check your local listings for times and stations in your area.

Believer's Voice of Victory Magazine

Enjoy inspired teaching and encouragement from Kenneth and Gloria Copeland and guest ministers each month in the *Believer's Voice of Victory* magazine. Also included are real-life testimonies of God's miraculous power and divine intervention in the lives of people just like you!

It's more than just a magazine—it's a ministry.

To receive a FREE subscription to
Believer's Voice of Victory, write to:

Kenneth Copeland Ministries
Fort Worth, TX 76192-0001
Or call:
800-600-7395
(7 a.m.-5 p.m. CT)
Or visit our Web site at:
www.kcm.org

If you are writing from outside the U.S., please contact the KCM office nearest you. Addresses for all Kenneth Copeland Ministries offices are listed on the previous pages.